Put Beginning Readers on the Right Track with
ALL ABOARD READING™

The All Aboard Reading series is especially for beginning readers. Written by noted authors and illustrated in full color, these are books that children really and truly *want* to read—books to excite their imagination, tickle their funny bone, expand their interests, and support their feelings. With four different reading levels, All Aboard Reading lets you choose which books are most appropriate for your children and their growing abilities.

Picture Readers—for Ages 3 to 5
Picture Readers have super-simple texts with many nouns appearing as rebus pictures. At the end of each book are 24 flash cards—on one side is the rebus picture; on the other side is the written-out word.

Level 1—for Preschool through First Grade Children
Level 1 books have very few lines per page, very large type, easy words, lots of repetition, and pictures with visual "cues" to help children figure out the words on the page.

Level 2—for First Grade to Third Grade Children
Level 2 books are printed in slightly smaller type than Level 1 books. The stories are more complex, but there is still lots of repetition in the text and many pictures. The sentences are quite simple and are broken up into short lines to make reading easier.

Level 3—for Second Grade through Third Grade Children
Level 3 books have considerably longer texts, use harder words and more complicated sentences.

All Aboard for happy reading!

To Aaron Kremin,
an original — P.D.

In memory of my dad — J.M.

Special thanks to Paul Dyer for photography —J.M.

Text copyright © 1993 by Patricia Demuth. Illustrations copyright © 1993 by Judith Moffatt. All rights reserved. Published by Grosset & Dunlap, Inc., which is a member of The Putnam & Grosset Group, New York. ALL ABOARD READING is a trademark of The Putnam & Grosset Group. GROSSET & DUNLAP is a trademark of Grosset & Dunlap, Inc. Published simultaneously in Canada. Printed in the U.S.A.

Library of Congress Cataloging-in-Publication Data
Demuth, Patricia. Snakes / by Patricia Demuth ; illustrated by Judith Moffatt.   p.   cm. — (All aboard reading) Summary: An introduction to an animal that's been with us since the time of the dinosaurs—the snake.   1. Snakes—Juvenile literature.   [1. Snakes.]   I. Moffatt, Judith, ill.   II. Title.   III. Series.   QL666.06D45 1993 597.96—dc20 92-24466   CIP   AC

ISBN 0-448-40514-8 (GB)   A B C D E F G H I J
ISBN 0-448-40513-X (pbk.)   C D E F G H I J

ALL
ABOARD
READING™
Level 2
Grades 1–3

Snakes

By Patricia Demuth

Illustrated by Judith Moffatt

Grosset & Dunlap • New York

Long, long ago,

before people knew how to write,

they drew pictures on cave walls—

pictures of animals.

About a million different animals

lived on Earth then.

But cave people drew only

a few of them.

The snake was one.

People have always

found snakes interesting.

Why?

Maybe it is their shape.

Snakes have no arms or legs.

Or maybe it is how they move.

Snakes slither and slide

on their bellies.

Or maybe it is their skin.
Snake skin is made up of
lots of little scales.
Most snake skin looks slimy,
but it isn't.
It is very dry.

There are over 2,400 kinds
of snakes in the world.
They come in many sizes.
The smallest is the thread snake—
no bigger than a worm.

The giant of all snakes

is the <u>anaconda</u>.

(You say it like this: an-a-CON-da.)

It can be as long as a school bus

and weigh as much as two grown men.

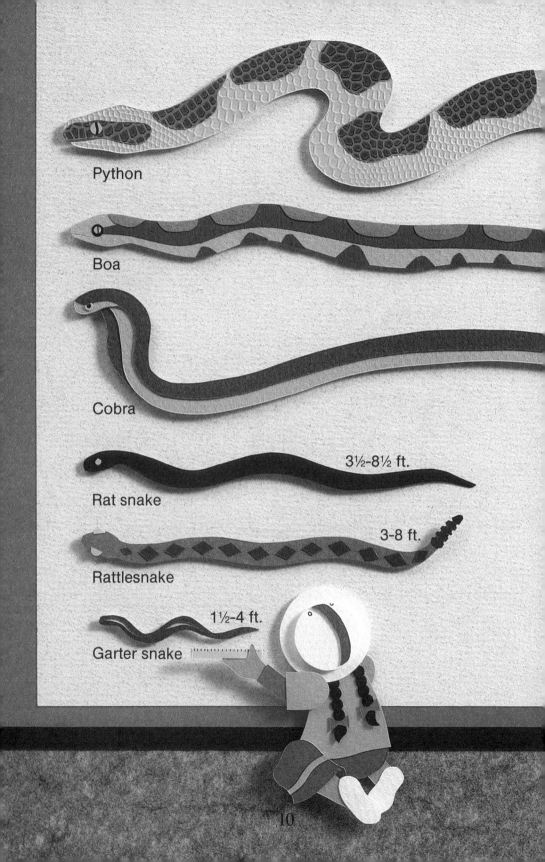

Python

Boa

Cobra

Rat snake

3½-8½ ft.

Rattlesnake

3-8 ft.

Garter snake

1½-4 ft.

10-30 ft.

6-18 ft.

8-18 ft.

Other snakes are somewhere in between.

Snakes live almost everywhere.

On land, in trees, and underground.

In the oceans and lakes.

But snakes don't live near

the North Pole or

the South Pole.

A snake's body can't make

its own heat like yours can.

So, cold air, cold snake.

But if the air is nice and warm,

then the snake is nice and warm, too.

Many kinds of snakes can live

through cold winters. How?

They find a warm place to hide—

in a deep hole, in a cave, or under rocks.

Then they go into a deep winter sleep.

Here they stay

until warm weather returns.

Even when snakes sleep,

their eyes are always open.

That's because they have no eyelids.

A clear cap covers each eye.

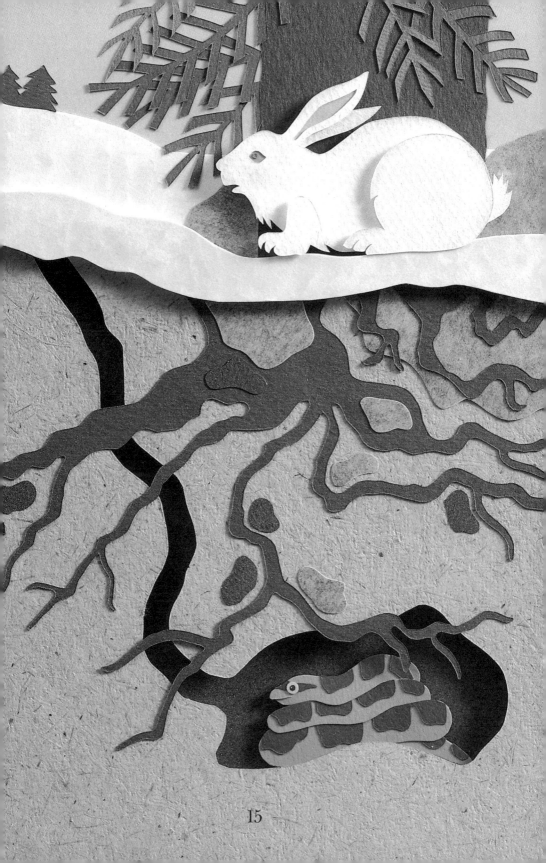

Most snakes don't see very well.

They can tell if something moves.

But this garter snake can barely see
the frog that is sitting so quiet and still.

Ribbit, ribbit.

The frog croaks.

The garter snake

cannot hear the frog.

Snakes have no outer ears.

The garter snake flicks its tongue
in and out.
Suddenly it can smell the frog!
Snakes pick up smells from the air
with their tongues.
A snake flicking its tongue is like
you sniffing with your nose!

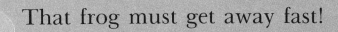
That frog must get away fast!

This is a rattlesnake.

A hungry rattlesnake!

Nearby a mouse hides.

The night is dark.

The rattlesnake cannot see

the mouse.

It is windy.

The wind carries away

the smell of the mouse.

How can the rattlesnake find

the mouse?

There are two holes

near each of its eyes.

They are called pits.

The pits can sense warmth.

They tell the rattlesnake that

a warm animal is close by.

In a flash, the rattlesnake

strikes the mouse.

It grabs it with its needle-sharp teeth.

Then it sinks its fangs into the mouse.

Poison flows through the fangs.

In seconds, the mouse is dead.

Are most snakes poisonous? No!

Many kinds of snakes

kill their prey by eating them alive.

Other kinds of snakes

kill their prey by squeezing!

This python is wrapping its body

around a wild pig.

When the python squeezes hard,

the pig can't breathe.

Snakes that kill prey by squeezing

are called <u>constrictors</u>.

(You say it like this: kon-STRICK-tors.)

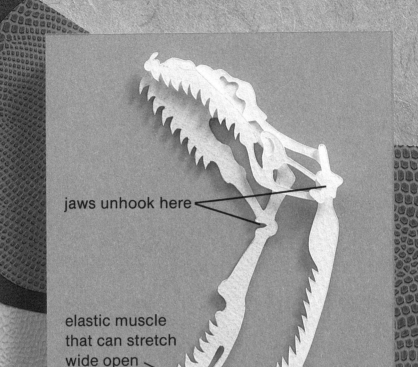

jaws unhook here

elastic muscle
that can stretch
wide open

Snakes do not chew their food.

They swallow it whole

by "unhooking" their jaws.

A python can swallow

a whole pig in one bite.

Slowly the python swallows the pig.
Later, the pig sits in one big lump
inside the snake.
A meal like this will last
the snake a long time.
It won't have to eat
for months!

This coral snake has stopped eating

for another reason.

Its eyes have turned cloudy blue.

These are signs that the snake

is ready to shed its skin.

The coral snake rubs its head

on a rock.

Rubbing breaks open the old skin.

Slowly, slowly,

the snake crawls out.

Snakes shed their skin

two or three times each year.

A new skin is all grown underneath.

The old skin is worn out.

The old skin peels off.

It comes off inside out,

like a T-shirt pulled over your head.

A snake is in danger
while it sheds its skin.
If an enemy comes,
the snake can't move
away quickly.
Several animals eat snakes—
hawks, eagles, skunks, foxes,
even other snakes!
So a snake needs ways
to protect itself.
Its skin colors help keep it safe.

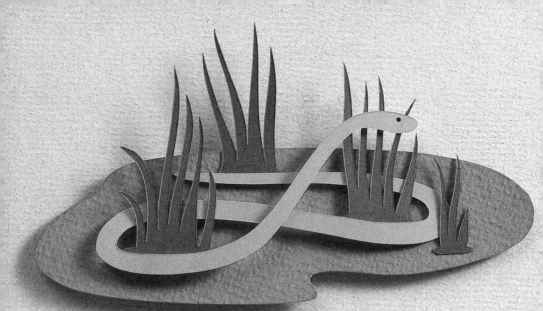

The green snake is the same color

as the grass.

The mud snake is hard to see

in the muddy swamp.

The sidewinder matches the color
of the desert sand.

Snakes protect themselves
in other ways, too.
A rattlesnake rattles its tail
to make a loud warning:
Ch-ch-ch-ch-ch!

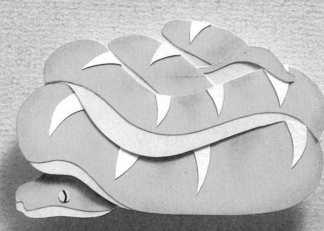

The boa curls up into a ball.

An enemy can bite its tail.

But the boa's head is still safe.

A cottonmouth opens its mouth

very, very wide.

Enemies flee from the scary sight.

An angry cobra

scares away enemies, too.

It rears up high.

It makes its neck big and flat.

It jabs forward

and gives a loud, sharp *hiss!*

Do snake charmers really charm cobras?

No.

The cobra rises out of its basket
to see what is going on.

Then the snake charmer
moves back and forth—
and the cobra just follows along!
But it can still be dangerous.

People are often scared of snakes.

And yet snakes help people.

They kill rats and mice

that eat crops.

And snake poison
is used for medicine.
Experts "milk" the fangs
to get out the drops.

People may fear snakes—
or they may like them.
But one thing is certain.
Snakes have been around
for millions
and millions
and millions of years.
Way before people, there were snakes.
Even back in the time of dinosaurs
there were snakes.

Snakes are here to stay!